Castle Terrace

Berwick's Grand Plan

for

Country Villas

George C. Murray & Karen McKenzie

GCM RECORDS LLP

First published 2020
By
GCM RECORDS LLP
Berwick Workspace
90 Marygate
Berwick upon Tweed
TD15 1BN
enquiries@gcmrecords.co.uk

Printed in the United Kingdom by Printspot (www.print-spot.co.uk)

978-1-913145-07-1

Cover image (reference BA/U6/1) showing *Cottage Hill* drawn on the proposed plan
drawn by William Smith (reproduced with permission from Berwick Records Office).

~ Acknowlegements ~

We are grateful to Linda Bankier, Berwick-upon-Tweed Archivist, and Friends of Berwick and District Museum and Archives for their valuable guidance during the process of researching this book.

Sources used in the book

Other than the sources which are referenced within the text and at the end of the book, the information contained in the book came from the following sources: Title Deeds and related documentation for 6 Castle Terrace, Census records, Berwick-upon-Tweed Guild Minute books (from 1833 – 1835), Berwick-upon-Tweed Council Minute Book (1836 onwards), The Town Clerk Guild Minute Book (1833 onwards), Minutes of the Berwick Board of Guardians and the newspapers The Berwick Advertiser, The Berwickshire News and General Advertiser, and The Windsor and Eton Express.

~ Contents ~

~ *Introduction* ~

Berwick-upon-Tweed has long been defined by its defensive walls. It is a town that has experienced many conflicts over the centuries and the town residents have sought relative safety behind the walls, whether the castle walls, the medieval walls or the more 'modern' Elizabethan walls. In the past few hundred years, following periods of stability and peace, Berwick residents felt sufficiently secure to settle outside of the walls. The development of villas outside of Berwick's walls represented a period of growth, prosperity and optimism in the town's history.

This is the story of Castle Terrace and what was to become a series of aspirational villas, built on the outskirts of Berwick. Developed on land that was previously used for farming, Castle Terrace grew up along the Dunse Road. This is also the story of two men, from markedly different backgrounds, who were instrumental in building the first two properties in this street: Luke Skelly, a saddler from Berwick, and Captain William Thomas Smith, an intrepid member of the Royal Navy, a man from an illustrious Northumbrian family heritage who later went on to be Mayor of the town.

Berwick-upon-Tweed

Berwick-upon-Tweed is a town steeped in history. Settlements in this area are evidenced back to Roman times and before, but Berwick itself was founded as an Anglo-Saxon settlement during the time of the Kingdom of Northumbria (654 – 954). In the 10th century, Northumbria was annexed by England and then in 1018 it was taken over by the Scots, following the Battle of Carham. Berwick Castle was built by David I of Scotland in the 1100s and was rebuilt in 1290. Berwick then changed hands between England and Scotland thirteen times between the years 1296 and 1482, when the English finally retook it. In 1551, the Elizabethan walls were built to protect Berwick from further invasion, but these were never used, and the town was left to grow and prosper.

Between 1611 and 1624, a stone bridge, which replaced the existing wooden bridge, was built across the river by order of King James. This linked the main route between Scotland and England. Between 1648 and 1652, the Holy Trinity Parish Church was built. The Barracks were built between 1717 and 1721 and the Town Hall between 1754 and 1760.

In 1820, the Union Bridge, the world's oldest surviving suspension bridge, was built five miles upstream from Berwick. In 1826, the Pier and the Lighthouse were completed and in 1836 the first house, *Cottage Hill*, was built in what was later to be known as Castle Terrace. Some years later in 1850, the Royal Border Bridge, designed by Robert Stevenson, was opened by Queen Victoria. Luke Skelly, owner of *Cottage Hill*, would have watched the construction of the 126-foot-high, 720-yard-long railway viaduct with 28 arches, from the front windows of his home.

Berwick in the 1800s

In the 1800s Berwick-upon-Tweed was a place of contrasting fortunes. The town had many thriving industries including shipping, iron foundaries, engine building, sacking, cotton hosiery, damask, diaper, carpets, hats and shoes. There was also substantial brewing and fishing. Ships of up to 500 tons could berth at the quay, as well as smacks and small brigs. The port experienced considerable trade in exports, such as corn, wool, salmon, cod, haddock, herring and coal. Imports included iron, hemp, tallow and bones for manure. There were markets on Wednesdays and Saturdays with a wide range of products including meat, vegetables and a variety of fish.

The population of Berwick-upon-Tweed was just under 9000 in the 1830s. There were clear areas of deprivation and poor housing in the town. Particular problems with sanitation were caused by the Elizabethan walls, as they blocked the drainage of foul water and sewage. In 1850, Robert Rawlinson provided a report to the General Board of Health on the sanitation condition of the inhabitants of Berwick-upon-Tweed. In this report, Mr Burnett, Superintendent of Works reported:

'The sewerage that exists in the town is very imperfect. There is no public sewer of any consequence but one in the town; this runs from the gaol down Hide-hill and Sandgate to the river where it discharges itself. It is, however, very shallow and too small.' (p22)

The main sewer was inadequate for the needs of the town population and flooded in wet weather, causing sewage to spill into the streets:

'The sewer from the new gaol in Wallace's-green to the river, is the principal one of the town, but is not sufficiently deep to allow the refuse from the Woolmarket to escape. It is so shallow that in wet weather it bursts through the street at the foot of Church-street, inundating Hide-hill; and a similar result takes place at the foot of Sandgate, where through the openings, it overflows the streets.' (p22)

This was further compounded by a lack of proper means of waste disposal. There were also sanitation problems caused by people keeping pigs on their properties, animals being slaughtered in the streets by butchers and waste from fish processing:

> 'I think the injurious effects caused by the collection of these heaps of manure are owing to the want of drainage, because, from there being no drain to carry away the dirty water and the filth of the houses, it is all thrown together, and the mixture of this with the ashes no doubt increases the offensiveness of these middens, and must contribute to the promotion of disease.' (p25)

This led to unsanitary conditions in the town and disease was prevalent with high incidences of typhoid, cholera and tuberculosis:

> 'I am personally acquainted with the state of the town generally. In those parts where disease has been the most prevalent it is in the most deplorable conditions. I have always found that if we have a foul district there disease is most prevalent, either in the form of Fever or Cholera. The existence of filth in one part of the town has also an effect on other parts causing scrofula.' [Scrofula is an old term for tuberculosis]. (p24)

The town suffered a series of cholera epidemics with, for example, a particularly bad outbreak in 1832 as documented by Rawlinson: 'In 1832 we had, I believe, 208 cases of Cholera, and upwards of 100 deaths.' (p27)

Many streets in the town had conditions that would suggest they were unfit for human habitation. Above Hide Hill in Wallace Green it was reported that: 'any drawing or written description can only convey a weak description of the actual neglect, filth, wretchedness, and misery palpable to sight and smell' (p17), while nearby in Church Street, a property is described as being: 'in an open drain the liquid refuse flows round the outer walls.' (p20)

Water Supply

The water supply to the town came from two main sources: 'The Ninewell Eyes' [water from springs and surface land drains] and 'The North Course' [surface catchment, conducted along a surface channel] (p28). There were: 'no impounding or filtering reservoirs for this water' (p28). Water was conducted to inhabitants by fountains or by public trough, with a pump or open spout attached. Most people had to travel a considerable distance to collect clean water and it could be in short supply in times of dry weather. Even the spring water could, however, become contaminated before reaching the town:

'At the springs the water is most beautiful; it is of the best quality; but one reason of its impurity I understand to be, that the farmers are allowed to drain their fields into the common watercourse.' (p29)

As well as the poor sanitation, the water supply could be further contaminated in the town with the open slaughtering of animals in the streets:

'Most of the butchers of the borough use some portion of their own premises as a place for slaughter and sheep are killed in the front of shop, open to the gaze of the public or on the side of the street. The inhabitants in the neighbourhood of these slaughterhouses complain very much of the nuisance created. The blood and refuse is allowed to accumulate and in summer decomposition takes place, and gases are given off highly injurious to health.' (p37)

In summary, Robert Rawlinson concludes:

'That excess of disease has been distinctly traced to the undrained and crowded districts, to deficient ventilation, and to the absence of a full water-supply, and of sewers and drains generally.' (p43)

The water supply was relatively unchanged since 1799, at which time Fuller, in his *History of Berwick-upon-Tweed*, describes the town water supply as being sourced from Cat Well near Letham Shank and New Farm Moor:

> '*After being joined by smaller springs, they meet at the south end of the Cow Close, and run in a stone conduit for about a quarter of a mile, when they enter wooden pipes, and discharge themselves into the reservoir at the foot of Castlegate. The length of the wooden pipes is about half a mile.*' (p477-478)

Overall, the 1850s sanitation report paints a grim picture of conditions in Berwick at the time, with disease and associated deaths being common.

Castle Terrace

Cottage Hill was the first house to be built in what is now known as Castle Terrace, however, its construction was not straightforward. Plans to develop a series of upmarket villas on the Dunse Road leading out of Berwick were drawn up by the architect, William Smith, and discussed by the Council in 1838, however, Luke Skelly had established *Cottage Hill* two years prior to this. This caused some consternation. His house did not comply with the plans and the building was not located exactly where it should have been as depicted by the architect's plans. If you look today, you can see that it is on a different alignment to the houses which were subsequently build next to it (see figure 1 overleaf).

Figure 1: Image (reference BA/U6/1) showing *Cottage Hill* as being out of alignment with the proposed plan drawn by William Smith (reproduced with permission from Berwick Records Office).

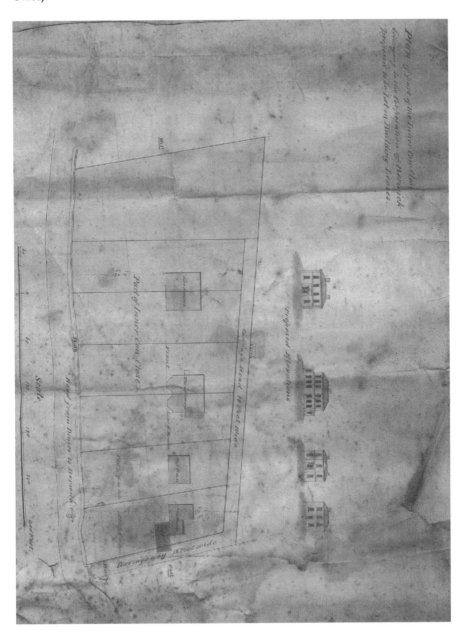

The Council debated whether the house should be demolished. Luke Skelly, however, was a determined man and defended his right to keep his house exactly where he had built it. The following sections outline the story of Luke Skelly, the man who built the first house on Castle Terrace and his new neighbour, the intrepid Captain Smith of Ava.

Luke Skelly and Cottage Hill

Prior to 1836, Luke Skelly was a saddler living in accommodation attached to his business premises on Hide Hill, which he rented from the Freemen. Hide Hill is mentioned in the 1850s sanitation report (Rawlinson, 1850) as a location that was subject to being flooded with effluent. Luke Skelly lived there with his younger sister, Isabella. Luke had previously run his saddler's business from these premises in partnership with his brother James. Unfortunately, James had died on the 12th November 1834, aged 54, leaving Luke to carry on the business himself.

No record could be found of either Luke or his brother ever having married, although Luke had a 'natural son,' called William Skelly, at some point. Isabella herself remained a spinster and their sister Alice, also a spinster, had also lived with them up until her death in 1821, aged 47. Their mother, Elizabeth had died soon after James on the 22nd December 1834, having reached the age of 88. Luke and Isabella's father, Rob, had died some years earlier in 1806, aged 63. Luke had lost a younger brother, also called James, who had died within a year of his birth, many years previously, when Luke was only eight. Isabella was the youngest of his siblings and was nineteen years his younger. In 1834, Luke was 63 years old.

As a saddler, Luke would have been aware of the growth of the railways. The Industrial Revolution had been a time of great change, but it was the implications of the expansion of the rail network that would, perhaps, have most perturbed him. The Stockton to Darlington Railway, the first public railway, had been opened in 1825 and the Rainhill Trials took place in October 1829. This was a competition where the winning locomotive would be chosen for service on the newly completed Liverpool and Manchester Railway.

There were five engines entered and the competition took place along a mile length of level track at Rainhill in Lancashire. The competition had a clear winner: 'The Rocket,' built by George Stephenson, which eclipsed all competition and the age of steam-powered transport had truly begun. Since the Rainhill trials, the proliferation of steam-powered transport was well underway, and it would not be long before Berwick would be swept up in its path, as had happened in other parts of the country. Luke would have most likely have read in the newspaper that the horse, as a form of transport, was on its way out, with the resultant threat to his livelihood.

In 1834, Luke began looking around the area for a suitable plot on which to build a new dwelling for himself and his sister. While the causes of death of his mother and brother are not recorded, they both died during a period of severe cholera outbreaks. On his death, James Skelly left all he had to his brother Luke, as stated in his Will.

It is possible that Luke wanted to escape from the stench of Hide Hill and to protect himself and Isabella, his remaining family member, from the risks associated with the recent cholera outbreaks. As a result, he focused his attention on a plot outside the main town. It is likely he had heard that Captain William Smith had been able to secure a building plot on farming land, that had been leased by Mr Robert Herriott from the Freemen, next to the Dunse Road. Robert Herriott, a farmer living in the Greenses, had an eleven-year lease on a plot of land and Captain Smith had an arrangement where he would continue to pay rent to Robert Herriott for the time remaining on his lease:

'This day All that Close or enclosed parcel of Land ground being Lot Number One of the Inner Cow Close is agreed to be demised to Mr Robert Herriott for the term of Eleven years from Michaelmas last at and under the yearly Rent of One Hundred and Eight Pounds and under and subject to Conditions as are entered in the Agreement Book which were read over in the Guilds previous to the letting thereof and whereunto the said Robert Herriott hath subscribed his name.' (Guild Minute Book, 16th October 1834)

The area referred to was just above the Old Mill, near Berwick Castle. It was also uncomfortably close to the Gallows Knowe where Grace Griffin had been publicly executed just twelve years previously, in 1823. The trial had caused a stir locally as, although Grace was accused of murdering her husband, he had been known to be a drunken wife-beater. The judge at the trial had made the jury aware of the circumstances. In addition, one of the witnesses was known to be unreliable, and the judge had, therefore, advised a more lenient disposal. Grace was, however, still found guilty and sentenced to hang. It had been more than fifty years since the previous execution and a new scaffold needed to be constructed.

The available land was essentially farmland, with few facilities, on the outskirts of town, however, there were many benefits from being located in an out of town area. There was the possibility of getting a connection to a nearby reservoir, thereby ensuring cleaner water. There would be fresh air and open spaces. In addition, the land outside the Walls was cheaper to lease. Luke Skelly must have been hoping for a similar arrangement to that given to Captain Smith and he wrote a letter to the Council to make his request:

'This Evening a Letter was presented to the Council from Mr Luke Skelly of the Borough, Saddler, making an application for a grant of a piece of Ground at the South end of the Cow Close in order to erect a Dwelling House thereon.' (Council Minute Book, 23rd February 1836)

Luke's request was successful, and it is recorded in the Council Minute Book that on the 3rd March 1836, the Petition of Mr Luke Skelly was granted on his producing consent of Tenant and plan of intended building:

Building Lease for 75 years granted Mr Luke Skelly at the rate of six pounds per acre per annum
'In pursuance of the order of the Council of the Third day of March last

on the Petition of Mr Luke Skelly, this Evening a plan of the intended
Building and the Tenant's consent thereto in writing was produced to the
Council and the Council having duly considered the same, it is ordered
that a Building Lease for Seventy Five years be granted to him at the rate
of Six pounds per acre per annum of a quarter of an acre more or less
of the First Lot of Cow Close occupied by Robert Herriott; such Rent to
be paid to the Tenant during the remainder of the Lease, and afterwards
to be paid to the Corporation during the residue of the said Seventy Five
Years.' (Council Minute Book, 22nd March 1836)

An application was subsequently made to the Lords of the Treasury to grant a lease extension to 300 years, which was also successful:

Application made to the Lords of the Treasury for leave to grant a Lease
of 300 years to Mr Luke Skelly.
'On Considering the Motion of Mr William Marshall It is ordered that
application be made to the Lords of the Treasury for granting a Lease of
300 years of a rood of Land to Mr Luke Skelly at the Yearly Rent of £1.
10. 0 for the purpose of building thereon a Dwelling House; according to
a plan to be produced and submitted to the Council.' (Council Minute
Book, 14th June 1836)

It is recorded in the Council Minute Book that on the 9th August 1836, that a letter from the Lords of the Treasury to the Mayor was read, acknowledging the receipt of the Memorial about the Grant of a Building Lease to Mr Luke Skelly. A letter from their Lordships was also sent calling for returns in answer to certain queries of which the following is a copy:

To the Mayor of Berwick

Sir,

Having laid before the Lords Commissioner of His Majesty's
Treasury the Letter from the Town Clerk of Berwick on the
27th June enclosing a Memorial from the Corporation of that
Town for permission to grant a Lease of Certain Land. I
have it in command to request you will cause my Lords to be
furnished with information on the following Points:

What is the estimated Annual expenditure of the Borough of
Berwick?
What is the amount of its Annual Income?
What is the Amount of any debt which may be owing by the
Corporation?
What is the Property now in the possession of the Corporation
and what may be its estimated value?

I am
Sir
Your Obedient Servant
J J Baring

Luke Skelly was pleased to discover that the Lords of the Treasury had sanctioned the granting of a three hundred-year lease. Unfortunately, things are rarely as straightforward as they initially seem and on 13th September 1836, a letter was sent noting that his house was out of alignment (see Figure 2 below), with the proposed plans for the area, which would be detrimental to any subsequent houses being built. As a result, he was ordered to knock down his house.

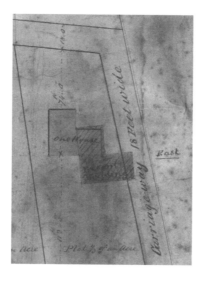

Figure 2: Image (reference BA/U6/1) showing a close-up of *Cottage Hill* as being out of alignment (reproduced with permission from Berwick Records Office).

Letter from the Treasury sanctioning Grant of a 300 Years Lease to Luke Skelly

'This day the Council took into Consideration a Letter received from the Treasury sanctioning the granting of a Building Lease for Three Hundred Years to Mr Luke Skelly of a Rood of Land situated in the Inner Cow Close. Also, the following report of the Committee of Works.

In consequence of a representation having been made to the Committee that the Site occupied by Mr Luke Skelly in the First Lot of Inner Cow Close would be detrimental to any future Buildings on the adjoining ground that may be afterwards erected. The Committee proceeded to view the same and are of the opinion that the site he has chosen is improperly placed And the Committee having examined the several orders of the Council made in this matter are of the Opinion that Mr Skelly has no authority as yet from the Council to proceed with the building and that the Town Clerk give him Notice to suspend any further proceedings the same until the Council give some further Order or Orders thereof.

And the Council having duly considered the same It is Ordered on the Motion of John Miller Dickson Esq and Seconded by Mr Ald. Dewar that the present House now building by Mr Skelly be taken down. And that if he chooses to replace it in the situation pointed out by Mr Smith Architect in his Plans (which was produced) he may do so on his previously entering into an engagement to produce a Plan of Specification for the same to be submitted for the approval of the Council And that the Town Clerk do write to Mr Skelly informing him thereof.' (Council Minute Book, 13th September 1836)

No further action takes place for six months, and Luke writes to the Council to chase things up:

> 'This Evening a letter from Mr Luke Skelly requesting that the Lease be granted him for Cottage Hill with the extension sanctioned by the Lords of the Treasury might be prepared for execution was laid before the Council and read.' (Council Minute Book, 13th March 1836)

Objections from some Council members remained. The Council was reconvened for a further meeting on the 20th March to resume the consideration of the letter from Luke Skelly presented at the last meeting. The Council records note that Mr Alderman Bogue, seconded by Mr John Cunningham, moved that the Lease requested by Mr Skelly be granted. John Miller Dickson Esquire, seconded by Mr John Tait, moved that the amendment should not be granted. Consequently, a division was resorted to. After a vote there were three votes in favour of the Amendment and five votes against. It was, therefore, ordered that the Lease requested by Luke Skelly be prepared accordingly:

<u>**Excerpt from: Proceedings of the Town Council –**</u>
<u>**Tuesday the 20th March 1838**</u>

The petition of Mr. Luke Skelly to have the lease of the building site granted him by the Council drawn out, was next read.

The Mayor supposed there would be no objection to this being granted.

Mr. Dickson said there was a considerable objection. The petitioner did not build his house according to stipulation; and on being remonstrated by a Committee appointed for the purpose, acted with great stubbornness. There is an order of Council entered in the book, requesting Mr. Skelly to desist building his house, as it had been represented that the spot selected by him would be detrimental to other persons building villas. Mr. Skelly paid no attention to that Committee, who even offered to refund the expense he had incurred, but continued to build his house in contempt of them. They wished him to build according to a plan furnished by Mr Smith.

Alderman Bogue – Mr. Smith's plan was not procured until Mr. Skelly had proceeded with the building the plan of which had been submitted to and approved of the Council. He moved that the petition be granted.

Mr. Cunningham seconded the motion.

Mr. Dickson – Mr. Skelly submitted the plan of the house, to which the Council assented, but did not specify the site selected. moved that the petition be rejected.

Mr. Tait seconded the amendment.

On division there appeared — for the motion, 5; against it, 3. The petition was therefore granted.

Mr. Dickson thought the Council had not used the committee well, who spent a considerable time have the matter arranged.

The Mayor thought the discussion would have the effect intended by Mr. Dickson, namely, a caution to those who contracted with the Council in being careful to fulfil their engagements.

(Berwick Advertiser, 24th March 1838)

On the 5th June 1838, the Council write to Luke Skelly:

'This Evening a Lease of part of the First Lot of Inner Cow Close to Mr Luke Skelly for Three Hundred Years was laid before the Council for execution. Ordered that the Committee of Works examine and report on the same at the Adjournment.' (Council Minute Book, 5th June 1836)

On the 19th June, Luke Skelly finally gets his lease:

> '*This Evening a lease of part of the First Lot of Inner Cow Close containing on quarter of an acre or thereabouts to Mr Luke Skelly for Three Hundred Years at the Yearly rent of One Pound ten Shillings was laid before the Council and the Town's Seal affixed thereto the Committee of Works having reported their approval of the same.*' (Council Minute Book, 19th June 1836)

Luke Skelly and his sister settle into life in their new home, *Cottage Hill*, situated on the Dunse Road, along with their twenty-year-old servant, Mary. *Cottage Hill* is the first house to be built on what is later to become Castle Terrace, considered by many to be the most prestigious street in Berwick upon Tweed.

Luke Skelly wrote his Will on the 13th February 1851, leaving everything to his sister, Isabella. He died, aged 83, on the 10th February 1854. He was buried in the Parish Church Cemetery, Berwick, alongside the rest of his family. His Will was proved in Durham on the 27th March 1854, and the house was left to his sister, Isabella. Isabella wrote her own Will on the 15th September 1859, and a codicil was added on the 23rd October 1874. Isabella died on the 8th May 1879, aged 89. She was buried in the Parish Church Cemetery next to Luke.

Following Isabella's death, the house was left to William Skelly. William Skelly did not live in the Berwick area, but worked as a saddler to the Queen in Windsor. William Skelly is described in Isabella's will as '*the natural son of my late brother, Luke Skelly.*' William Skelly put *Cottage Hill* up for sale and it was advertised for sale via public auction:

'DESIRABLE RESIDENCE FOR SALE, CASTLE TERRACE, BERWICK-UPON-TWEED. Mr. MILLER *will offer for* SALE *by Public Auction, on* THURSDAY, 26th *day of June,* 1879, *in the* KING'S ARMS ASSEMBLY ROOM, BERWICK-UPON-TWEED, *at* TWO *o'clock afternoon prompt.*

ALL that DWELLING HOUSE and OFFICES with large Garden situate Castle Terrace, Berwick-upon-Tweed, known as Cottage Hill, long occupied by the late Miss Skelly. The premises comprise a quarter of an acre of Ground held under a Lease from the Mayor, Aldermen and Burgesses of the Borough of Berwick-upon-Tweed, for a term of 300 years, from the 22nd day of March, 1836, at the annual rent of £1.10s. Further particulars and leave to view may be had on application to the Auctioneer, Bridge Street, or to James Gray, Solicitor, Berwick-upon-Tweed.' (Berwickshire News and General Advertiser, Tuesday 24th June 1879)

The house is quickly sold, for the sum of £710:

'Sale of Property – On Thursday afternoon, the sale took place of the Dwelling House and Offices with large garden, situate at Castle Terrace, Berwick-upon-Tweed, known as Cottage Hill, long occupied by the late Miss Skelly. The premises comprise quarter of an acre of ground held under a lease from the Mayor, Aldermen and Burgesses of the borough of Berwick-upon-Tweed, for a term of 300 years, from the 22nd day March 1836, at the annual rent of £1.10s. Bidding commenced at £400, and after spirited competition, it was knocked down to Councillor Hopper at £710. Mr James Gray was the solicitor for the seller, and Mr A. L. Miller discharged the duties of auctioneer.' (Berwickshire News and General Advertiser, Tuesday 1st July 1879)

On the 2nd August 1879, the document of sale is signed transferring ownership of *Cottage Hill* from William Skelly to Mr Christopher Hopper.

Captain Smith and Ava House

The second property to be built, in what was to become Castle Terrace, was constructed by Captain William Thomas Smith. Captain Smith had acquired his lease prior to Luke Skelly, but *Cottage Hill* was built first. Captain Smith came from a very different background to that of Luke Skelly. He was born in 1791, second son of Thomas Smith and Ann Carr. Thomas Smith was from West Thirston, Northumberland.

Ann Carr was born in the town of Sunbury in Georgia, America. Her grandfather, Mark Carr, had played a significant role in the establishment of Georgia as a colony. He was originally from Eshott, Northumberland, but had travelled to America as an Officer with General James Oglethorpe's Regiment in 1738. He took with him his three children, William Carr, Judith Carr and Thomas Carr (Ann Carr's father). Mark Carr was involved in a number of endeavours including building forts and battling with the native Indians, the Spanish, and the French. He was rewarded for his exploits by being awarded land by the King and he set up a plantation from which he made his fortune.

Ann Carr's mother died giving birth to her. Ann returned to England with her father in 1772. The situation in America had become untenable with tensions rising in the years leading up to the American War of Independence, which began in 1775. Ann Carr married Thomas Smith on the 30th August 1787, in Felton, Northumberland.

In 1805, Captain Smith joined the Navy. Between 1805 and 1815 he was on Military Service in Europe. On 1st June 1813, Captain Smith began serving under Capt. P B N Broke on *The Shannon*, which captures the American ship *The Chesapeake*. In 1815, he was appointed to *The Tiber*. Between 1824 and 1826, he was on Military Service in India. On December 1825, he was appointed to *The Alligator* and the following year he was in command of the launch belonging to the *Boadicea*, which took part in the capture of Mellone. Promotion to the rank of Commander followed in 1826.

The next year, Captain Smith was married to Isabella Wilson in

Berwick-upon-Tweed. Their first two sons, William Thomas Smith and William 'Berry' Smith were born in 1828 and 1829 respectively at Ovingham, Northumberland. The next three children were born in Berwick-upon-Tweed: Elizabeth Anna Smith was born in 1832, Dr Philip Broke Smith was born on the 18th July 1834, and John Wilson Smith was born in 1838. Captain Smith looked to create a home for his family. He found a plot of land at the corner of Dunse Road and North Road in Berwick on land that was, at the time, rented as farming land by the Freemen. He writes to the Guild asking for permission to build on the site:

'This day Capt. Smith R N presented a petition to the Guild stating that he was desirous to erect a Dwelling House with suitable outbuildings and grounds on that part of Calf Hill Close which adjoins the Road leading to Dunse provided he was granted a lease of the requisite quantity of Ground That he had had the same surveyed and that an account of the irregularity of the boundary line between the close and the Road and the acuteness of the angle of the South Corner and the unevenness of the ground there, it appeared that in order to render the said site convenient for the purpose it would be requisite that it should extend in front from the Cow Close to the said angle And paying the Guild to grant him a lease for 500 years of the said piece of Ground and a line drawn from the Cow Close Wall at a point distant Sixty yards from where that wall meets the fence between the said Calf Close and the Dunse Road at a yearly Rent of Six Pounds per acre with liberty to straighten the line of fence between it and the Dunse Road in such a manner as may lawfully be done with the consent of the Turnpike Trustees, and also with the privilege of laying down a water pipe in communication with the Reservoir on the Calf Hill.'
(Guild Minute Book, 16th February 1835)

The Guild grant Captain Smith a lease for a 500-year period:

<u>Petition of Capt. Smith Granted</u>
'Ordered on the Petition of Captain Smith R N that he be granted a Lease for Five Hundred Years of a portion of the Calf Hill Close according to the terms of the petition, on his agreeing with the Corporation Tenant of that Close for the same.' (Guild Minute Book, 12th March 1835)

The agreement is sealed at the yearly rent of seven pounds and ten shillings:

'This day the following leases were Sealed. A Lease to Captain Smith R N of an acre and a quarter of Ground on the South Side of the Calf Hill Close for the term of Five Hundred Years at the Yearly Rent of Seven Pounds ten shillings.' (Guild Minute Book, 26th March 1835)

Captain Smith highlights things he would like to change about the site and offers solutions to the Guild which he feels would be of mutual benefit:

'This day William Smith Esquire R N presented a Petition to the Guild stating that it would be a Public Advantage and improvement if the Acute corner of the Cow Close Wall (near the Gateway) which so inconveniently projects into the Turnpike Road were rounded off, and the line of the fence gradually brought into Conjunction with the Western Extremity of his intended Wall and the entrance to the Cow Close made a little further to the West where the Turnpike Road is somewhat wider And the said petition also stated that such alteration would not be in any way advantage to him except that it would enable him to terminate his wall more neatly than adhering to the present plan and in consideration of that he would make such alteration of his own expense.' (Guild Minute Book, 4th May 1835)

The proposals put forward by Captain Smith to the Guild are accepted:

The petition of Capt. Smith R N about the improvement on the acute corner of The Cow Close Wall Granted.
'This day the Guild also took into consideration the Petition of Capt. Smith R N presented and read at last Guild about the improvement of the acute corner of the Cow Close Wall he intending making it at his own expense provided the Guild agreed thereto And the Guild having duly considered the same It is ordered that the prayer of the said petition be granted and that the School Committee be and they are hereby empowered to see the same carried into effect by Capt. Smith at his own expense.' (Guild Minute Book, 14th May 1835)

Captain Smith establishes his property and names it *Ava House*. It is thought that the name refers to the ancient Kingdom of Ava in Burma (now Myanmar). Ava was the capital of Upper Burma until 1555 and was destroyed by earthquakes on 23rd March 1839, the year *Ava House* was built. Captain Smith had served in this area during his career in the Royal Navy. Captain Smith lived in *Ava House* with his wife Isabella and their children. In April 1842, his son, Dr Henry Robert Smith was born. Captain Smith became Mayor of Berwick and served as a Justice of the Peace. Captain Smith died on the 6th October 1862, aged 72. The Berwick Advertiser printed an obituary to him:

THE LATE CAPTAIN SMITH OF AVA
'ILL would it become us to allow so distinguished officer and so excellent a man to pass away without a tribute to his memory. Rich to overflow as are the annals of the British Navy In deeds of heroism and gallant daring it would difficult point to a more illustrious career than that of Captain Smith. The following notice of his professional career appears in the Naval and Military Gazette:
"He entered the Navy in July 1806 a first class volunteer on board 'The Shannon' of 50 guns, under the command Captain Philip Broke.

In that frigate, after visiting the Greenland Seas for the protection of the whale fisheries, witnessed the surrender of Madeira, and assisted as midshipman in taking, among other vessels, 'Le Pommereuil;' French cutter, privateer, of 14 guns and 60 men; 'The Nautilus' American brig of 14 guns and 106 men; and 'The Thorn' privateer 18 guns and 140 men. He was also, on the 1st June, 1813, present at the memorable capture of the American ship 'Chesapeake' of 50 guns, yielding broadside 690 lbs. and 376 men — an exploit which was achieved after fifteen minutes of intense combat, productive of a loss to the British 24 men killed and 59 wounded, and to the enemy of 47 killed and 115 wounded. Chesapeake's maintop was stormed by Midshipman William Smith and his topmen, about five in number, who either destroyed or drove deck all the Americans there stationed. This gallant youth had deliberately passed along the Shannon's foreyard, which was braced up the Chesapeake's mainyard, which was nearly square, and thence into her top.

"As a reward for the valour he had displayed, Mr Smith, who had been particularly recommended by his Captain, was promoted the following 14th July to the rank of Lieutenant. He continued in the 'Shannon' till November 1813; and was subsequently appointed, 27th October, 1815, to 'The Tiber,' 38 guns. Captain Dacres, with whom served on the Irish, Newfoundland, and Channel stations until paid off. 18th September 1818, and in May 1822 and December 1825 to 'The Alligator,' 28 guns. Captains Thomas Alexander and Henry D. Chads; and 'Boadicea 46 guns', Commodore Sir James Brisbane, both in the East Indies, where he was actively employed during the war in Ava. While attached to 'The Alligator,' he commanded a division boat, in February 1825, at the destruction of a stockade a few miles above Thesit. He contrived about the same period to render ineffective several of the enemy's powerful fire rafts, and was in strongest manner eulogized Brigadier- General Cotton for the gallantry and judgment with which conducted the light division boats in an attack made upon an extensive stockade at Paulang. In the ensuing April, after having further distinguished himself in command of breaching battery in operations against Donoohew, we find him mentioned for his exertions the boats superintending the passage across the river Irawady. Sir Archibald Campbell's advanced guard, consisting two European regiments. In September, 1825 he was employed as negotiator at Meady, in conjunction with Lieut. Colonel Tidy; on 2nd December following he contributed to the capture of nearly 300 boats, laden with arms, ammunition, grain, and military stores, and on the 5th he assisted in completing the discomfiture of the Burmese army. On the 26th he was again selected to act in the character of a diplomatist. In command of the launch belonging to the Boadicea Capt. Smith shared in the capture of Mellone, 12th Jan. 1826. He was subsequently, with the light division his orders, active in annoying the enemy's outposts. Being advanced for his services to the rank of Commander, 22nd July 1826, he was employed in that capacity from 14th April, 1831, until paid off 16th September, 1833, in 'The Philomel' 10 guns, in the Mediterranean: from 26th June 1835 until 1838, in the Coast Guard; and from 9th August, 1841, until the close of 1844 in 'The Syren' 16 guns, in the East Indies. He attained his rank of Post Captain, 13th March, 1846."

And yet after such a career of honour and glory Captain Smith never reached a higher rank than that of Post Captain: it is true now as when Shakespeare wrote the lines —

"* Tis as the curse of service:
Promotion goes by favour"

The tide victory from their greater weight of metal had been long running in favour of the Americans, and at the decisive fight between 'The Shannon' and 'The Chesapeake,' so confident were the Americans, that they had prepared a banquet and a ball to greet their countrymen on their return from an assured victory; we may imagine, therefore. what was their consternation when they observed 'The Chesapeake' being towed along by 'The Shannon' and carried to Halifax.

When his wars were over Captain Smith built a house which he called Ava, and which looked over the element he loved so well.

31

He became Mayor of Berwick, and was in 1845, appointed a Justice of the Peace by Commission from the Crown. At the weekly meeting of the Magistrates, if the Mayor for the time being was not present, (who presided ex-efficio) Captain Smith was always voted into the chair. As a magistrate his conduct was characterised by practical good sense. He held the scales of justice with an even hand and an impartial hand, and his sifting of conflicting and contradictory evidence pointed out his fitness for such an office. He was one of the Trustees the Grammar School, and for several years had been annually elected their chairman.

His death was not merely an individual but a public loss. His interment was attended the officers and seamen the coast guard and the gunboat 'Ruby,' by the Mayor and Magistrates, the Recorder and Sheriff, and by the members of the Burial Board and Harbour Commission, and Trustees of the Grammar School.

Over the coffin was laid the union Jack, and it was borne to the cemetery by the sailors attached to the navy, the whole being witnessed by crowd of sympathising spectators. And if this record of his life shall make his worth more extensively known the object the writer will have been attained. No man more richly deserved, than Captain Smith did, that the inscription "Palman qui meruit ferat", let him bear the palm who has deserved it, should be applied to him — H. G. C. Clarke.

Captain Smith was born Thirston, his father's estate in Northumberland, but resided in this town for upwards of twenty years prior his decease, and, during that period, had filled all the chief civic offices of the borough. Mayor (three occasions), Sheriff, Alderman, & c. At the time of his death was a Justice the Peace, and chairman of several public bodies, the Harbour Commissioners, Burial Board, Trustees of the Grammar School, & c.

Whether considered in his public capacity, or his social station, no one in this town more commanded and secured the confidence and regard of the entire community. He was distinguished alike for his high sense of honour, strict impartiality, and sound judgement, and for his warmth of heart and courtesy of manner.

His loss will be long and severely felt among us:

"A good man is a public good."

The remains of Captain Smith were interred on Friday last in the new cemetery with public honours.'

(Berwick Advertiser, 18th November 1862)

Following her husband's death, Isabella moved to Southsea where she lived until her death, aged 91, on 27th February 1886. She was buried there. *Ava House* was subsequently sold to James Allen, Timber Merchant.

Castle Terrace – A Grand Plan for Country Villas

It seems that Luke Skelly and Captain Smith, although from very different backgrounds, were ahead of their time in developing the first of the grand villas on the Dunse Road, using strips of land that had been previously rented from the Guild as farmland. Architect, William Smith's plan for the area was not tabled and discussed until 1838 and *Cottage Hill* was built and plans for *Ava House* were already well under way by this time. Captain Smith had acquired his plot in 1835 and Luke Skelly had acquired his in 1836. Luke Skelly did not waste any time in getting *Cottage Hill* built and *Ava House* was established by 1839. Captain Smith's lease had more favourable terms than those given to Luke Skelly and *Ava House* was a much grander development.

It appears that *Cottage Hill* was built primarily as a family home, whereas Captain Smith's house was designed to be more reflective of his status. Luke Skelly had to fight to get a more favourable lease and was eventually successful in doing so. He also had to fight to prevent his beloved new home from being knocked down following a dispute about whether it had been correctly sited on the plot leased to him. Again, his doggedness paid off and the house stood. Little is known about how the neighbours got on with each other, but there is a hint that Luke Skelly was undaunted by the wealth and status of Captain Smith in the minutes of the Berwick Board of Guardians:

'A letter from Mr Luke Skelly was read out complaining of a nuisance being caused by a pig kept on Captain Smith's premises.' (Minutes of the Berwick Board of Guardians, 29th October, 1849)

Following the building of *Cottage Hill* in 1836 and *Ava House* in 1839, there was a hiatus in the development of further properties along the Dunse Road on the land previously rented for farming by the Freemen. Figure 3 shows the vacant plots of land adjacent to *Cottage Hill* in 1852.

Figure 3: Vacant plots adjacent to *Cottage Hill* from Ordnance Survey Town plan of Berwick-Upon-Tweed surveyed 1852 (reproduced with the kind permission of the National Library of Scotland)

Other properties existed in the area, including *Calf Hill Farm House* on the North Road and *Castle Hills House*, which was built by the Askew family in the 1830s. The lull in development was despite the existence of the plan developed in 1838 by Mr William Smith, Architect: '*Plan of Part of the Inner Cow Close belonging to the Corporation of Berwick proposed to be let as Building Leases.*' This plan included the already existing *Cottage Hill*, plus three other properties next to it on the north side of the Dunse Road. The plans included a single detached property at what is now 8 Castle Terrace, followed by two further semi-detached properties, all according to the model of upmarket villas.

The *Toll House* at the start of the Dunse Road is thought to have been built between 1847 and 1851, but the development of the villas stalled. It is not clear why there was a hiatus, but further grand villas were not begun until the 1850s and the houses that were subsequently built do not match up with those originally planned by William Smith. Eventually, as we can see today, a series of grand villas were built throughout the Victorian era, offering houses that provided the style that had previously only been available in out of town country houses.

Two detached villas were built at what are now numbers 14 and 16 Castle Terrace. Following this, in 1855, *Hopeville*, was built on the site next to *Cottage Hill*, at what is now 8 Castle Terrace, and a further detached villa was constructed in 1857, at what is now number 18. On the other side of the Dunse Road, *St Mary's Vicarage* began construction in 1859. In the 1860s, semi-detached properties were constructed in the remaining space, at what are now 10 and 12 Castle Terrace, and further up the road at what are now numbers 20 and 22. A series of grand villas continued to be developed throughout the Victorian period on the north side of Castle Terrace. Six similar semi-detached properties (1, 3, 5, 7, 9 and 11 Castle Terrace) were developed in 1890, as well as three other large properties at numbers 15, 17 and 19. There were further periods of development on the south side in the 1930s and 1970s and houses were also later developed in plots in the grounds of *Ava House*.

Castle Terrace has continued to undergo development, with plots being built upon up until the present day. There is now an eclectic mixture of styles of houses, each representing the period in which it was built. The area to the north of Berwick has also been extensively developed and Castle Terrace is no longer a street out on its own and the houses are no longer referred to as country villas.

The site at what would have been 21 Castle Terrace remains undeveloped following the discovery of the remains of a medieval church and graveyard. The remains date back to a time in the thirteenth century when the area had been settled and was a part of a village called Bondington. During the Border wars, however, it was no longer a safe place to live and people moved back within the town walls, abandoning the area.

Today *Cottage Hill* still stands as the first house built in what has become Castle Terrace. At some point in its history it was renamed 'The Old Farmhouse,' but there is little evidence to suggest that the house ever served this function. The building has been extended and reconfigured on the inside, but the original external footprint of the building remains intact. It now also has a garage behind the house, but the layout of the gardens is largely unchanged from the original design.

Ava House still stands at the junction of Dunse Road and the Edinburgh Road (Castle Terrace and North Road). At some point in its history it was renamed *Ava Lodge*. Much of its grounds have been lost to housing development and the name *Ava Lodge* represents the addresses of a cul-de-sac of numbered houses as well as the name of the house itself. At the time of writing *Ava Lodge* is an office for a firm of accountants, rather than being a grand home for a family of status.

To a large extent, Castle Terrace realised architect William Smith's original plan for a series of grand country villas on the outskirts of town, but the street also represents the extension of that vision, with the construction of many grand buildings situated in large grounds, that were built for the well-heeled inhabitants of the town at the time.

Two men, however, were ahead of this plan: Captain Smith building a grand country house that would eventually become *Ava Lodge* and Luke Skelly building a family home for himself and his sister, perhaps to escape the sanitation issues and disease within the Walls of Berwick. We can only speculate how well these two men got on as neighbours, but we do know that Luke Skelly once complained to the Corporation about Captain Smith's pig. After his many years in the Royal Navy, with his involvement in so many theatres of conflict, we can but imagine how he might have felt about the stubborn saddler from Berwick complaining about his animal husbandry.

Appendix: People in this Book

Luke Skelly: born in Berwick upon Tweed in 1772, Saddler, lived with family in Hide Hill prior to the building of *Cottage Hill*, died in Berwick-upon-Tweed on the 10th February 1854, aged 83, buried in the Parish Church Cemetery, Berwick-upon-Tweed.

Isabella Skelly: sister of Luke Skelly and fellow inhabitant of *Cottage Hill* after living with rest of family in Hide Hill, born in Berwick-upon-Tweed in 1791, died in Berwick upon Tweed on the 8th May 1879, aged 89, buried in the Parish Church Cemetery, Berwick-upon-Tweed.

James Skelly: brother and business partner of Luke Skelly, Saddler, born in Berwick-upon-Tweed in 1780, lived with family in Hide Hill, died in Berwick-upon-Tweed on the 12th November 1834, aged 54, buried in the Parish Church Cemetery, Berwick-upon-Tweed.

Alice Skelly: sister of Luke Skelly, born in Berwick-upon-Tweed in 1774, lived with family in Hide Hill, died in Berwick upon Tweed on the 10th July 1821, aged 47, buried in the Parish Church Cemetery, Berwick upon Tweed.

Elizabeth Skelly: mother of Luke Skelly, born in Berwick-upon-Tweed in 1746, lived with family in Hide Hill following the death of her husband, Rob, died in Berwick-upon-Tweed on the 22nd December 1834, aged 88, buried in the Parish Church Cemetery, Berwick-upon-Tweed.

Robert (Rob) Skelly: father of Luke Skelly, born in Berwick-upon-Tweed in 1743, Butcher, died in Berwick upon Tweed on the 2nd December 1806, aged 63, buried in the Parish Church Cemetery, Berwick-upon-Tweed.

James Skelly: brother of Luke Skelly, born in Berwick-upon-Tweed in January 1778, died in Berwick-upon-Tweed on 19th June 1778, aged 6 months, buried in the Parish Church Cemetery, Berwick-upon-Tweed.

William Skelly: Natural son of Luke Skelly, Saddler to the Queen in Windsor.

Captain William Thomas Smith: born in West Thirston, Northumberland in 1791, Royal Navy, lived in Ava House, died in Berwick-upon-Tweed on 6th October 1862, buried in Berwick Cemetery.

Thomas Smith: father of Captain Smith, born in 1747 in West Thirston, died in August 1826 in Felton, Northumberland.

Ann Carr: mother of Captain Smith, born on the 22nd January 1765 in Georgia, America, died on the 25th May 1806 in West Thirston, Northumberland.

Mark Carr: great-grandfather of Captain Smith, born in Eshott, Northumberland in March 1702, fifth son of William Carr (1658 – 1738), died in 1767 in Turtle River, Parish of St Patrick, Georgia, America.

Thomas Carr: grandfather of Captain Smith, born in Brampton, Yorkshire, 1733, travelled to America with his father Mark Carr and his brother and sister, William Carr and Judith Carr, died on the 16th December 1793 in Brinkheugh, Northumberland.

William Carr: son of Mark Carr, born in 1730 and travelled to America with his brother Thomas Carr and his sister Judith Carr, died in 1770 in Georgia, America.

Judith Carr: daughter of Mark Carr, born in 1732 and travelled to America with her brothers, Thomas and William Carr, died in 1771 in Georgia, America.

Thomas Smith: grandfather of Captain Smith, born in 1720 in Togston, Northumberland, died in West Thirston in 1765.

Ann Carr: grandmother of Captain Smith, born in 1743, dies after giving birth to Captain Smith's mother, Ann Carr, in 1765 in Sunbury, Georgia, America.

Isabella Wilson: wife of Captain Smith, born in 1795, daughter of John Wilson, died 27th February 1896 in Southsea, Hampshire.

William Thomas Smith: son of Captain Smith, born in 1828 in Ovingham, Northumberland.

William "Berry" Smith: son of Captain Smith, born in 1829 in Ovingham.

Elizabeth Ann Smith: daughter of Captain Smith, born in 1832 in Berwick-upon-Tweed, died in 1885.

Philip Broke Smith: son of Captain Smith, born on the 18th July 1834 in Berwick-upon-Tweed, died in 1905.

John Wilson Smith: son of Captain Smith, born in 1838 in Berwick-upon-Tweed.

Dr Henry Robert Smith: son of Captain Smith, born in April 1842 in Berwick-upon-Tweed, died in 1916.

Robert Herriott: born in Scotland, Farmer, lived in The Greenses, Berwick-upon-Tweed, rented farmland in Inner Cow Close, died in Berwick-upon-Tweed in 1847, aged 70, buried in the Parish Church Cemetery, Berwick-upon-Tweed.

General James Oglethorpe: born 22nd December 1696, died 30th June 1785, buried The Parish of All Saints Cranham, Upminster, Soldier, Member of Parliament and Founder of the colony of Georgia.

References

Fuller, J. (1799). *The History of Berwick-upon-Tweed: Including a Short Account of the Villages of Tweedmouth and Spittal.* Ulan Press.

Johnston, T. (1817). *The History of Berwick-upon-Tweed and its Vicinity.* Berwick: Printed by H. Richardson for John Reed and John Wilson.

Rawlinson, R. (1850). *Report to the General Board of Health on a Preliminary Inquiry into the Sewerage, Drainage, and Supply of Water, and the Sanitation Condition of the Inhabitants, of the Parish of Berwick-upon-Tweed, in the County of the Borough and Town of the same, including the Townships of Tweedmouth and Spittal.*